EVERYTHING
IS TEMPORARY

EVERYTHING IS TEMPORARY

Illustrated Contemplations

on How Death Shapes Our Lives

IRIS GOTTLIEB

A TARCHERPERIGEE BOOK

an imprint of Penguin Random House LLC
penguinrandomhouse.com

Most TarcherPerigee books are available at special quantity discounts for bulk purchase for sales promotions, premiums, fund-raising, and educational needs. Special books or book excerpts also can be created to fit specific needs. For details, write: SpecialMarkets@penguinrandomhouse.com.

Library of Congress Cataloging-in-Publication Data
Names: Gottlieb, Iris, author.
Title: Everything is temporary: illustrated contemplations on how death shapes our lives / Iris Gottlieb.
Description: New York: TarcherPerigee, [2022]
Identifiers: LCCN 2022005495 (print) | LCCN 2022005496 (ebook) |
ISBN 9780593419472 (trade paperback) | ISBN 9780593419489 (epub)
Subjects: LCSH: Death—Social aspects. | Death—Social aspects—Pictorial works.
Classification: LCC HQ1073.G68 2022 (print) | LCC HQ1073 (ebook) |
DDC 306.9—dc23/eng/20220210
LC record available at https://lccn.loc.gov/2022005495
LC ebook record available at https://lccn.loc.gov/2022005496

Printed in the United States of America
1st Printing

Book design by Shannon Nicole Plunkett

For everyone, dead or alive, human or not.

And, as always, for Bunny.

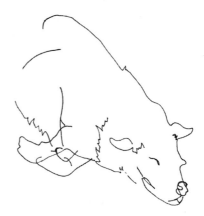

YOU EXISTED LONG BEFORE YOU
WERE BORN, IN THE DNA OF YOUR
ANCESTORS

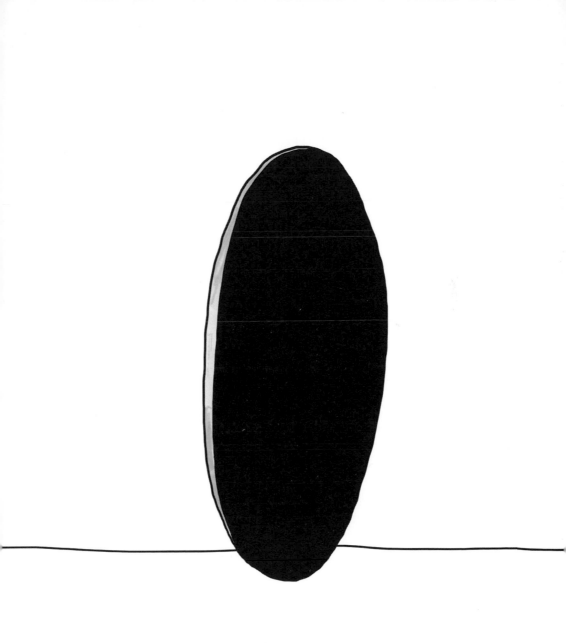

FROM THE SECOND AFTER YOU WERE
BORN ONWARD, THERE WILL NEVER BE
A TIME IN WHICH YOU DO NOT EXIST

WE
ALL
HAVE
FEARS

SOME OF US AVOID

THINKING ABOUT DEATH

AND SOME OF US ARE UNABLE
TO MOVE THROUGH LIVING
BECAUSE WE'RE TOO
AFRAID OF DYING

SOME OF US MAKE SMALL
ALTARS FOR THE LIVING AS
REASSURANCE WE'LL HAVE
ARTIFACTS OF THEIR PRESENCE
IN OUR LIVES IN CASE THEY
DIE

MUSEUM OF ARTIFACTS GIVEN OR MADE
BY A LIVING PARTNER

YOU ARE ALREADY DYING.
YOU ALWAYS HAVE BEEN.

WE ALL HAVE.

THERE IS AN ANCIENT CONCEPT
CALLED "MEMENTO MORI," WHICH
TRANSLATES TO

"REMEMBER THAT YOU DIE."

IT HAS BEEN A PRACTICE AMONG
PEOPLE THROUGHOUT HISTORY TO
ACTIVELY THINK ABOUT, ACKNOWLEDGE,
MEDITATE ON, AND LIVE WITH THE
KNOWLEDGE THAT WE ALL DIE.

DEATH AWARENESS HAS BEEN A
NORMAL PART OF CULTURES AND
RELIGIONS AS A WAY TO ORIENT
OURSELVES IN OUR LIVES—THE MORE
MINDFUL OUR RELATIONSHIP IS
WITH DYING, THE DEEPER OUR
RELATIONSHIP WITH LIFE CAN BE.

"CONSIDERING DEATH"

BUT IN MODERN SOCIETY, WE REFUSE TO TALK
HONESTLY ABOUT THE TRUTH THAT WE ALL WILL
DIE, AND SO WE HAVE DENIED OURSELVES THE
RIGHT TO DIE WITH HONOR AND CARE.

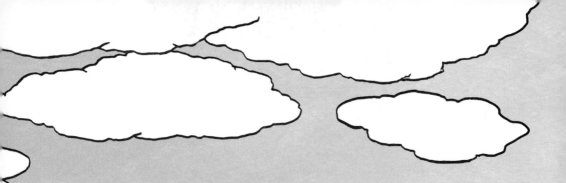

INSTEAD, WE HAVE RELEGATED THE PROCESS OUT OF OUR HOMES, OUT OF SIGHT AND SILENCED FROM CONVERSATION.

WE CAUSE MORE PAIN, MORE HARM, AND MORE PERSONAL AND SOCIETAL STRUGGLE BY DENYING THE REALITY OF OUR MORTALITY.

WE TALK ABOUT GRIEF, ITS STEPS AND STAGES, BUT THE EXPERIENCE OF GRIEF IS NEITHER LINEAR NOR UNIVERSAL.

WE CAN CAUSE OURSELVES MORE PAIN BY ONLY DEALING WITH GRIEF AFTER DEATH HAS HAPPENED RATHER THAN BEGINNING THE PROCESS OF GRIEF WITH PEOPLE WHILE WE'RE STILL ALIVE.

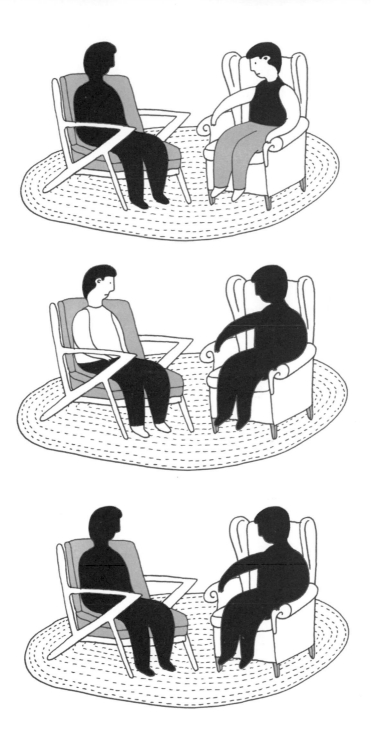

EVERY BODY IS IN THE PROCESS OF DYING AND IT'S OK.

SINCE WE'RE ALREADY ON THE JOURNEY TOWARDS DEATH, THE BEST WE CAN DO IS FIND PEACE AND CONTENTMENT WITH THE DESTINATION.

WE DON'T WANT TO MEET A TOTAL
STRANGER WHEN WE GET THERE.

HOW WOULD IT FEEL TO THINK OF DEATH
NOT AS A WEIGHT THAT WILL PULL US OUT
OF LIFE

BUT MORE AS A SUPPORT THAT WILL
CARRY US TOWARDS REST?

IF YOU COULD MEET DEATH, WHAT WOULD YOU ASK?

ABOUT THE WORKINGS OF THE UNIVERSE?

ABOUT ITS FAVORITE FORMER PLANETS?

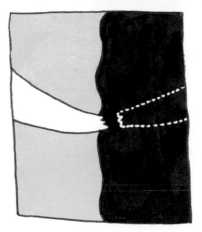

ABOUT THE UNFAIRNESS OF WHO AND HOW?

OR

WHERE ARE THE
MEMORIES OF
PEOPLE WHO DIE?

HOW DO WE,
THE LIVING, CARRY
SOMEONE WITH US
IF OUR MEMORIES
OF THEM FADE?

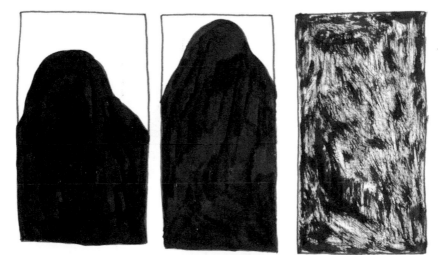

WHAT'S IN THE MOMENT JUST BEYOND?

THERE IS SOME COMFORT IN KNOWING THAT NO ONE WILL EVER BE ABLE TO EXPLAIN WHAT BEING DEAD IS LIKE.

WHILE THE UNKNOWN IS FEAR-INDUCING, WHAT IF YOU FOUND OUT WHAT HAPPENS AND IT WAS

DISAPPOINTING?

OR TERRIFYING?

OR WONDERFUL?

HOW WOULD IT CHANGE YOUR LIFE TO KNOW AHEAD OF TIME?

MAYBE THERE ARE PEOPLE CLAPPING
AND SMILING FOR US WHEN WE LEAVE
THIS BODY.

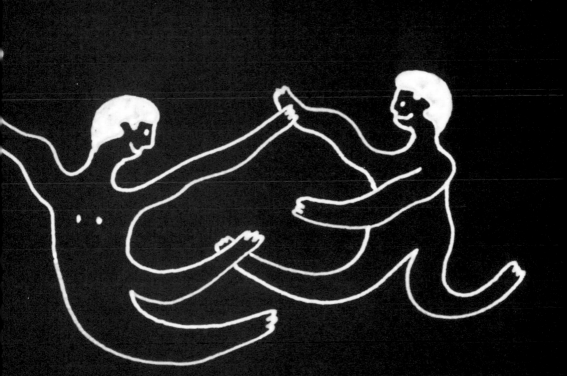

MAYBE WE SEE EACH OTHER AGAIN.

MAYBE THERE IS
TRULY NOTHING.

MAYBE WE BECOME
GHOSTS OR SPIRITS.

MAYBE WE'RE STILL ALIVE IN ANOTHER UNIVERSE

OR WE BECOME BABIES AGAIN AND START OVER IN OUR SAME LIVES WITH THE ABILITY TO DO IT DIFFERENTLY

OR WE BECOME
PLANTS IN THE WOODS.

MAYBE WE JUST BECOME MEMORIES
THAT LEAVE THE EARTH WHEN EACH
PERSON WHO REMEMBERED US DIES.

MAYBE WE CAN
ACCEPT THAT
ONCE WE ARE

GONE FROM OUR
BODY, WE ARE GONE
FROM OUR BODY.

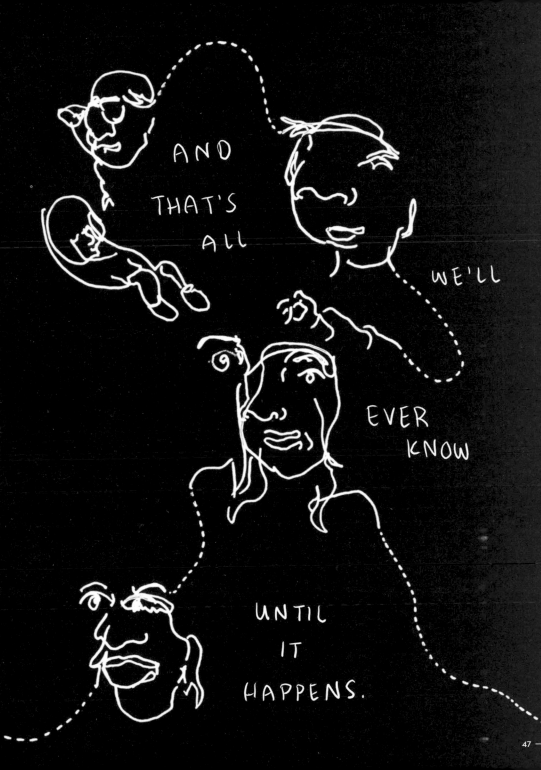

WHEN YOU THINK ABOUT DEATH AND THE TRANSITION
FROM LIVING TO DEAD, WHAT DOES THAT LOOK LIKE TO YOU?

IS IT THE LAST BREATH TAKEN?

THE LAST HEARTBEAT?

IS IT A SPECIFIC MOMENT AT ALL?

IT'S IMPOSSIBLE TO IMAGINE NO LONGER EXISTING.

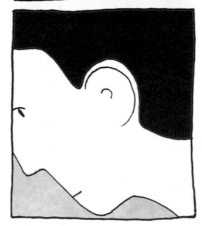

WE CANNOT EXPERIENCE UNCONSCIOUSNESS, AND DEATH IS ETERNAL UNCONSCIOUSNESS.

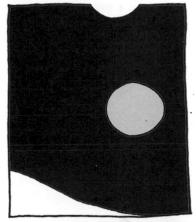

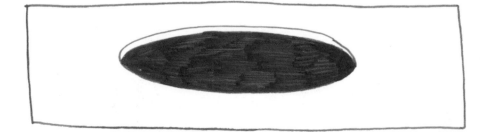

THERE ISN'T A UNIVERSALLY AGREED-UPON DEFINITION OF DEATH,

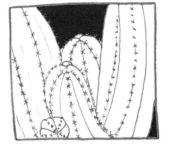

SINCE ALL ORGANISMS FUNCTION DIFFERENTLY WITHIN OUR CRITERIA OF BEING ALIVE.

THE CESSATION OF

HEARTBEAT, BREATH, OR CONSCIOUSNESS

ARE ALL CONSIDERED DEFINING
FEATURES OF DEATH FOR HUMANS,

BUT WHAT ABOUT THE DEATHS OF
ORGANISMS THAT HAVE NO HEART,
LUNGS, OR KNOWN CONSCIOUSNESS?

HOW DOES THAT
CHANGE

OUR METRIC OF DEFINING DEATH?

DEATH IS A PROCESS

NOT AN
EVENT

WE CAN FEEL DEATH
WITHIN OURSELVES

LOSING
THE ABILITY
TO CONNECT
WITH OTHERS

LOSING
LOVED ONES

LOSING
A SENSE
OF SELF

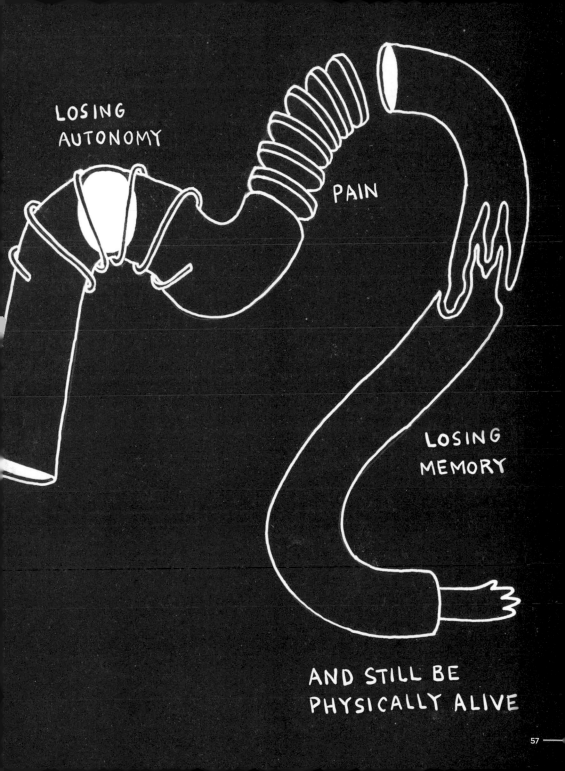

AS WE DIE, OUR BODIES TURN OFF THEIR LIGHTS. FOR SOME, THE POWER SHUTS OFF WITHOUT WARNING, AND FOR OTHERS, IT'S A SLOWER PROCESS OF DIMMING WHAT WAS ONCE BRIGHT, ROOM BY ROOM, UNTIL ALL IS STILL AND DARK.

OUR LIVES AND DEATHS ARE
INFINITELY SMALL AND INSIGNIFICANT
IN THE SCOPE OF THE UNIVERSE.
OUR PLANET IS YOUNG, HUMANITY IS FAR
YOUNGER, AND OUR LIVES ARE MERE
MOMENTS ON THE SCALE OF TIME.

HOW DO WE
FIND MEANING IN
OUR LIVES AND OUR
DEATHS, KNOWING
THAT WE ARE SUCH A
SMALL MOMENT IN THE
SCOPE OF THE
UNIVERSE?

PEOPLE ARE ENAMORED
WITH THE IDEA

THAT WE ARE
"MADE OF STAR STUFF."

ISN'T BEING MADE OF EARTH
STUFF EVEN MORE AMAZING?

WE ARE MADE OF THE SAME MATERIAL AS PLANTS, OCEANS, INSECTS, AND THE ATMOSPHERE.

AND YET, WE ARE MORE DRAWN
TO THE IDEA THAT WE COME FROM
SOMEWHERE WE HAVE NEVER BEEN,
FROM A TIME BEFORE
WE EVER EXISTED.

WE ARE MADE OF THE EARTH,
AND WHILE OUR PHYSICAL
FORMS RETURN TO THE EARTH,

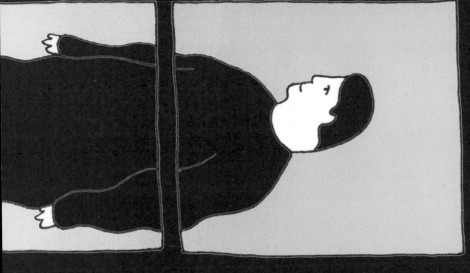

WE ARE OFTEN AFRAID OF
WHERE OUR SOULS, SPIRITS,
US-NESS MIGHT GO.

MAYBE THERE IS A SPIRIT OR SOUL THAT EXISTS BEYOND THE LIFE OF A BODY, AN EXTENSION OF SELF TO A TIME OR PLACE BEYOND WHERE WE ARE NOW. OR MAYBE WE SEEK PEOPLE'S SPIRITS WHEN WE NEED TO ASSURE OURSELVES THAT DEATH ISN'T SO SCARY.

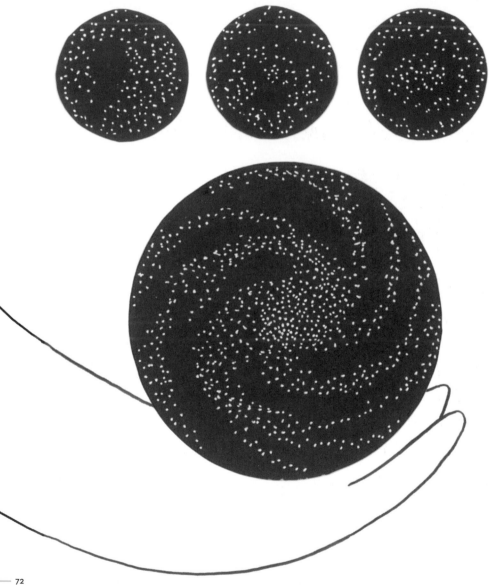

SOME FIND IT COMFORTING THAT THE PEOPLE WE LOVE MIGHT EXIST SOMEWHERE NOT FAR FROM US, AND THEREFORE WE WON'T HAVE TO BE FAR FROM THE PEOPLE WE LOVE WHEN WE DIE.

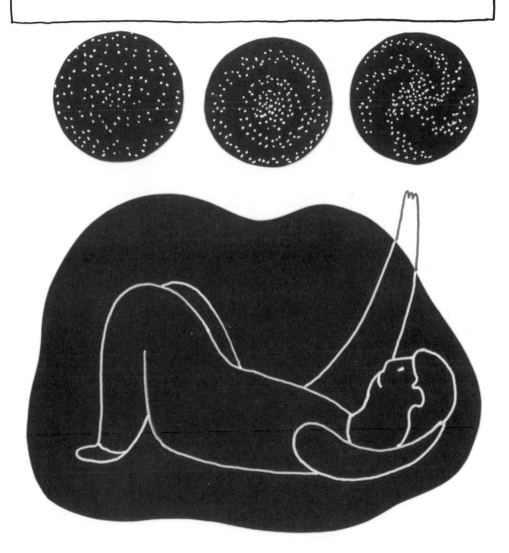

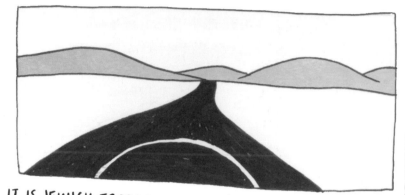

IT IS JEWISH TRADITION TO LEAVE STONES ON GRAVES.

THE ORIGIN OF THE PRACTICE IS UNKNOWN.

IT POSSIBLY EVOLVED FROM SHEPHERDS KEEPING

PEBBLES TO COUNT THEIR SHEEP AND HAS MORPHED INTO A RECORD OF VISITORS PASSING THROUGH.

IT MIGHT BE TO KEEP THE SOULS OF THE DEAD BURIED WITH THE BODIES BY MAKING A BARRIER.

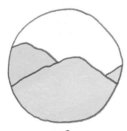

OR

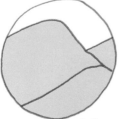

BECAUSE

LIVING

THINGS

WEREN'T

ABUNDANT

IN

THE

DESERT.

IT MIGHT'VE BEEN TO MAINTAIN ROCK PILES THAT INDICATED GRAVE SITES.

STONES ARE PERMANENT. THEY DO NOT HAVE THE BREVITY OF FLOWERS OR FOOD COMMONLY LEFT AS HOMAGE TO THE DEAD. A STONE MIGHT REPRESENT AN EVERLASTING BOND BETWEEN THE LIVING AND THE DEAD.

AND EVENTUALLY, EVERY STONE LEFT
BY THE LIVING WILL BE THEIR
PERMANENT MARK—THEIR BOND
TO THE LIVING WORLD.

PLANTS AND FUNGI

BECOME FOOD FOR ANIMALS

LIVE IN THE FOREST OR

BE THE FOREST

WOULD WE BE LESS AVERSE TO THE
IDEA OF DECOMPOSING IF WE WERE
CONSUMED BY DIFFERENT CREATURES?

OR WOULD WE BE LESS AVERSE TO THOSE
CREATURES IF WE WEREN'T EATEN
BY THEM?

SOMEONE INVENTED A SUIT FULL
OF FUNGI SPORES THAT GROW WHEN
A CORPSE IS BURIED IN IT.

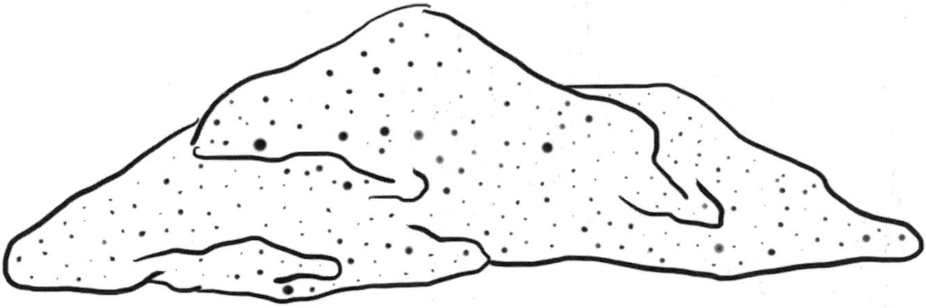

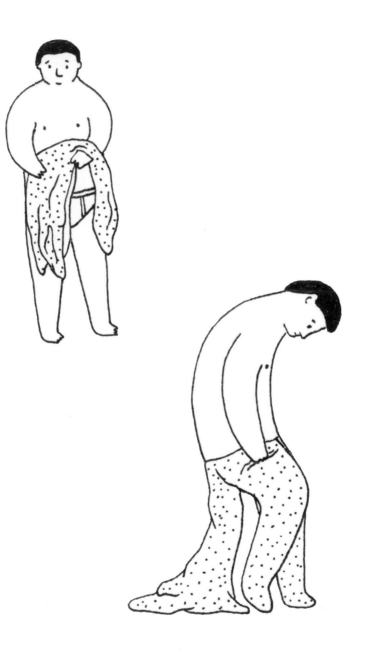

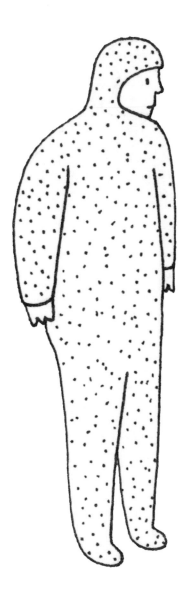

THERE ARE SO MANY WAYS OF
TREATING THE
BODY WHEN IT
DIES.

BURIAL,

ALLOWING
ANIMALS TO
CONSUME IT,

CANNIBALIZING IT,

BURNING IT.

IN SOME WAYS OUR EMOTIONAL
REACTIONS TO DIFFERENT
TREATMENTS OF A DEAD BODY
REFLECT OUR OWN FEELINGS
ABOUT HOW WE WANT OUR
BODIES TO BE TREATED, HONORED,
AND RESPECTED.

THE BO PEOPLE OF SOUTHERN CHINA HUNG
COFFINS FROM CLIFF FACES HUNDREDS OF
FEET ABOVE THE GROUND. THEY WERE
MOST LIKELY KILLED OFF DURING THE MING
DYNASTY IN THE 1500s AND NO RECORDS
REMAIN ABOUT WHY THE DEAD WERE PLACED
THERE, BUT FOR MORE THAN 3000 YEARS

SOME OF
THE DEAD
HAVE BEEN
PRESERVED
IN THE SKY.

IN TIBET, THERE ARE SKY BURIALS.

BODIES ARE PLACED HIGH IN
THE MOUNTAINS TO BE EATEN
BY VULTURES.

VULTURES HOLD CEREMONIES FOR THE DEAD.

THEY WEAR BLACK.

THEY GATHER AND THEN

THEY HANDLE THE BODY OF THE DEAD.

SCAVENGERS AND DECOMPOSERS HAVE EVOLVED TO SURVIVE OFF THE DEAD AND RECYCLE THEIR BODIES

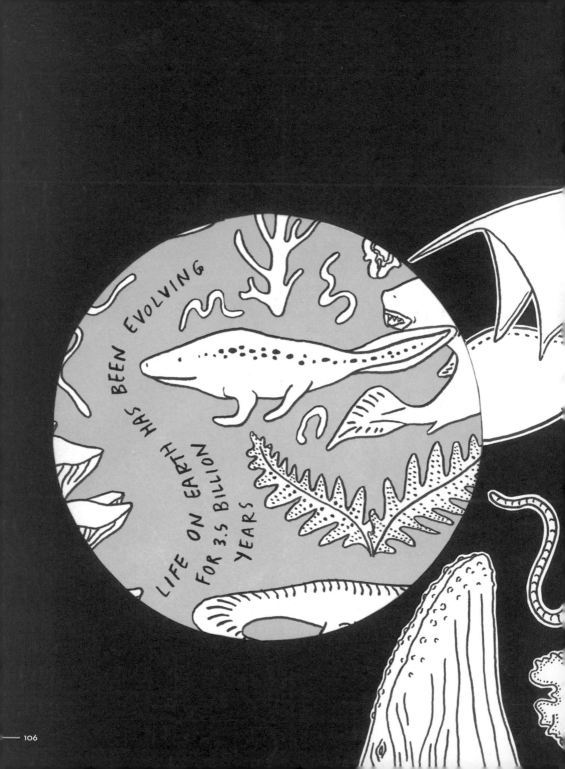

AND DEATH HAS SHAPED WHAT LIFE ON EARTH LOOKS LIKE

IT HAS GIVEN US THE
OPPORTUNITY FOR EVOLUTION,
CHANGE, AND GROWTH TO
EXIST. OVER 100 BILLION
PEOPLE HAVE DIED SINCE THE
FIRST HUMANS EVOLVED. WE
WOULD HAVE NEVER EVOLVED
TO BE WHO WE ARE WITHOUT
THE DEATHS OF BILLIONS
OF BEINGS, OF ALL
SPECIES, BEFORE US.

WE DRIVE CARS THAT RUN ON FUEL CREATED BY THE
DEATHS OF DINOSAURS 65 MILLION YEARS AGO.

WE, AS HUMANS, ARE IN
THE UNIQUE POSITION OF
KNOWING WE WILL DIE.

MAYBE WE HAVE
CONVINCED OURSELVES
THAT WE ARE SO SEPARATE
FROM THE NATURAL WORLD
THAT TO FULLY BECOME
INDISTINGUISHABLE FROM
IT IN DEATH WOULD
THREATEN OUR ILLUSIONS
OF SUPERIORITY

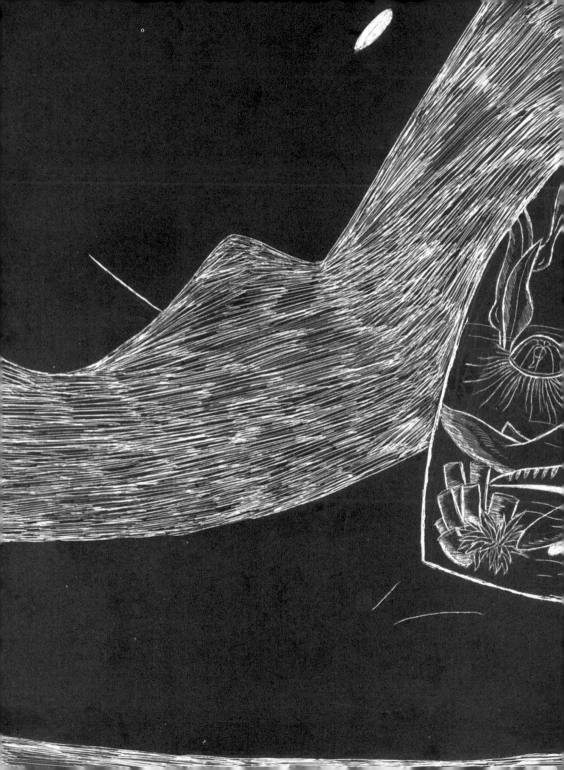

ALMOST EVERY ANIMAL ON EARTH IS GRANTED APPROXIMATELY 1.5 BILLION HEARTBEATS IN A LIFETIME.

HUMANS AND CHICKENS ARE
THE OUTLIERS WITH ABOUT
2-2.5 BILLION.

BECAUSE OF THIS,
WE (AND MAYBE CHICKENS) HAVE
TRICKED OURSELVES INTO

BELIEVING WE
ARE DIFFERENT,

THAT WE CAN OUTRUN
DEATH BY LIVING LONGER,

BEING STRONGER,

ALTERING OUR BODIES
BEYOND THEIR
HUMAN LIMITS.

BUT THE BODY IS
MEANT TO
DIE.

IT'S DESIGNED THAT WAY,
AND DEATH IS ULTIMATELY
A NECESSARY PART OF
THE CONTINUATION OF LIFE
ON EARTH BEYOND OURSELVES.

-238°

WE WANT TO BE
REMEMBERED.

MANY OF US SPEND A LOT OF
OUR LIVES WORKING TOWARDS
CREATING AN IMPACT

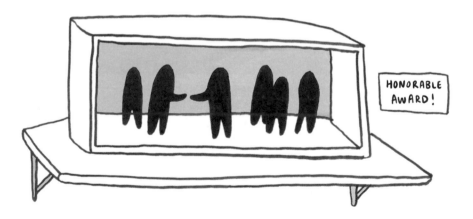

SOME FOR THE SELFLESS
BETTERMENT OF THE WORLD

AND SOME TO ASSURE OURSELVES THAT
WE WERE IMPORTANT, WORTH
REMEMBERING.

WE EQUATE LEGACY WITH THE
VALUE OF LIFE, BUT WHEN WE'RE DEAD,
WE PROBABLY WON'T CARE IF WE'RE
REMEMBERED OR NOT.

EVEN IF YOU MANAGE
TO ARRIVE AT A PLACE OF
TRUE ACCEPTANCE OF DEATH,
EXPERIENCING THE DEATH OF OTHERS
AND YOUR OWN CAN STILL BE
AGONIZING AND DEEPLY SORROWFUL.

ACCEPTING THE INEVITABILITY OF DEATH
DOESN'T MEAN BEING UNAFFECTED BY
IT. BEING AWARE AND THOUGHTFUL
ABOUT OUR LIMITED TIME ON EARTH
DOESN'T NECCESSARILY MAKE
LOSS LESS PAINFUL, BUT IT MIGHT.
EASE THE FEAR OR BETTER
PREPARE US TO GRIEVE.

ONE OF THE HARDEST AND MOST HOPEFUL
THINGS ABOUT DEATH IS THAT LIFE ALL
AROUND IT CONTINUES FORWARD. IT IS HARD
BECAUSE WE MUST LEARN TO LIVE WITHOUT
SOMEONE OR SOMETHING AND KNOW THAT
PEOPLE WILL CONTINUE ON IN THEIR LIVES
WITHOUT US.

BUT IT IS HOPEFUL THAT PEOPLE FIND
WAYS TO HEAL AFTER LOSS, FIND ONE
ANOTHER THROUGH SHARED LOSS, WHILE
THE PLANET, INDIFFERENT TO US,
CONTINUES SPINNING AND LIVING.

TIME STEADILY MOVES

AND CARRIES US ALONG UNTIL OUR LIFE IS OVER.

AND IT KEEPS ON GOING

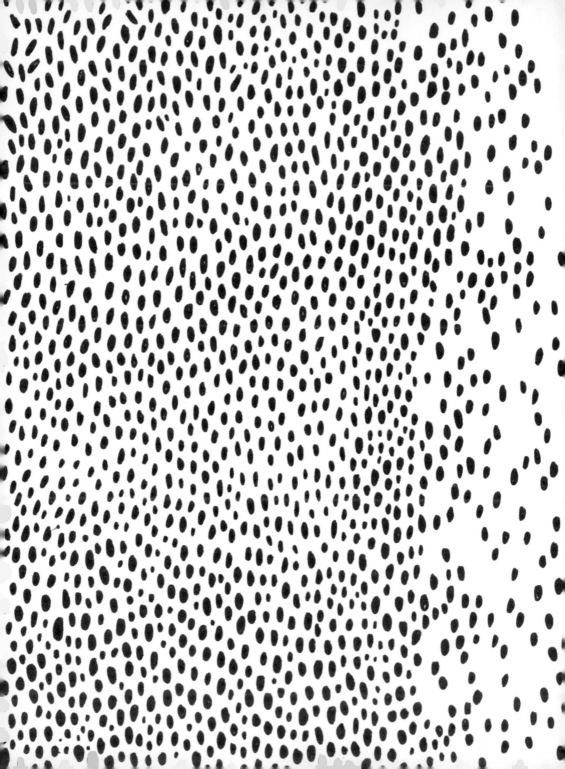

OVER

TIME

PEOPLE

WILL

LEAVE

OUR

LIVES

MEMORIES FADE.

WE ARE GRIEVING ALL THE TIME

IN WAYS WE MIGHT NOT IDENTIFY AS
PRACTICES IN GRIEF.

WE GRIEVE THE LOSS
OF RELATIONSHIPS,

IMPORTANT
OBJECTS,

FAMILIAR PLACES,

THINGS WE AREN'T ABLE
TO EXPERIENCE.

MORE OFTEN THAN NOT,
GRIEVING AND LOSS
CREATE CHANGE:

INTERRUPTIONS OF
NORMALCY,

SHIFTS IN PERSPECTIVE, AND

RESHAPED IDENTITIES.

GRIEVING CAN BE FILLED WITH SORROW,

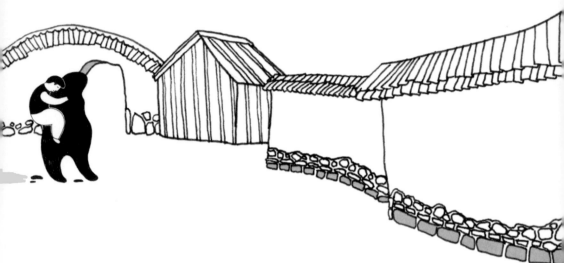

YET IT SIMULTANEOUSLY USHERS US
TOWARDS DEEPER UNDERSTANDINGS OF
TEMPORALITY AND OUR LACK OF CONTROL.

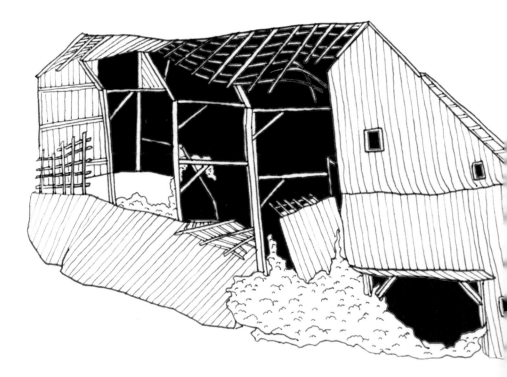

SOMETIMES WE LET THINGS
DIE PASSIVELY.

SOMETIMES WE HAVE TO
DECIDE WHEN SOMETHING DIES.

WHEN DEATH BECOMES ISOLATED
AND SHUT AWAY, IT BECOMES
INVISIBLE, EASY TO IGNORE.

IN THESE SETTINGS, OUR AGENCY
OVER OUR LIVES AND DEATHS
IS OFTEN TAKEN AWAY.

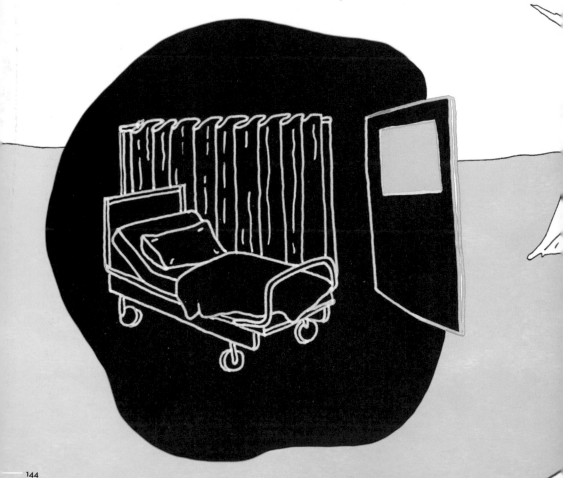

IT'S COMMON TO PERFORM DRASTIC MEDICAL PROCEDURES TO KEEP DYING PEOPLE ALIVE, OFTEN TO THE DETRIMENT OF THEIR OWN LIFE.

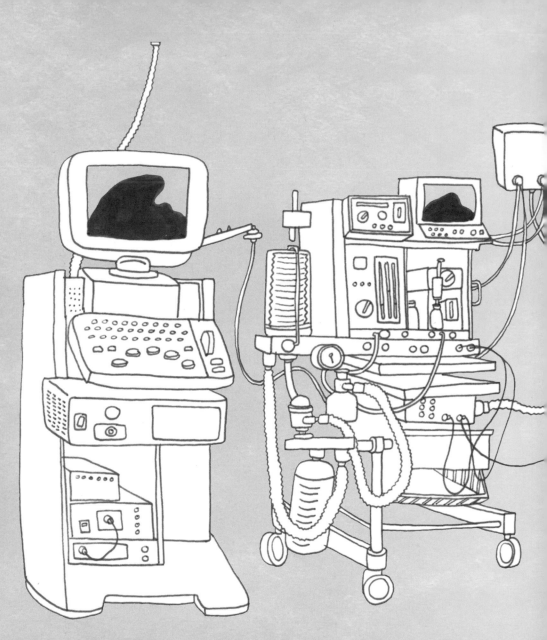

WE CAN BE PUT INTO A POSITION OF BEING
KEPT ALIVE BY MACHINES AND MEDICATIONS,
AND WE CAN BE DRAWN TO THE NOTION

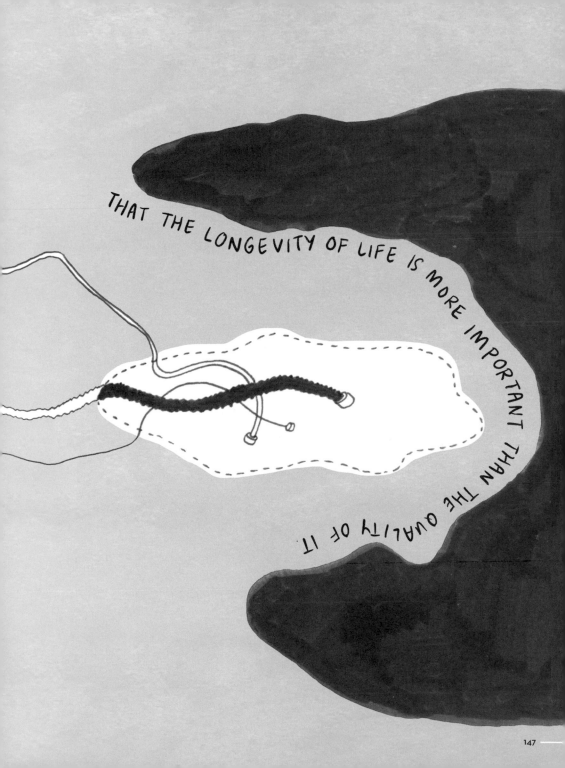

THAT THE LONGEVITY OF LIFE IS MORE IMPORTANT THAN THE QUALITY OF IT

IT IS GRADUALLY BECOMING MORE ACCEPTABLE THAT, SHOULD OUR DEATH BE PROLONGED AND PAINFUL, WE SHOULD HAVE CONTROL OF OUR COMFORT, QUALITY OF LIFE, AND QUALITY OF DEATH WITH THE ASSISTANCE OF MEDICAL PROFESSIONALS.

MAKING THE CHOICE TO DIE TO PREVENT PROLONGED
SUFFERING FROM TERMINAL ILLNESS OR OLD AGE IS A
RADICAL ACT OF ACCEPTANCE OF MORTALITY AND LETTING
GO. THIS DOESN'T MEAN IT'S A DEATH THAT'S WELCOMED
OR DESIRED, BUT ONE THAT, GIVEN THE SITUATION, ALLOWS
FOR THE MOST AUTONOMY FOR THE DYING.

WHEN DO WE KNOW THAT WE'RE READY?

HOW DO WE RESPECT THOSE WHO ARE READY

WHEN WE WANT THEM TO STAY?

MAYBE IT COMES DOWN TO TRUST AND INTUITION THAT THE TIME IS RIGHT

OF COURSE, NOT EVERYONE HAS THE OPPORTUNITY TO DIE WITH SUPPORT AND CARE.
SOME LIVES ARE TAKEN BY OUTSIDE FORCES WITH NO ABILITY TO DECIDE THE CIRCUMSTANCES.

LOSING SOMEONE UNEXPECTEDLY FORCES US TO CONFRONT THE LACK OF CONTROL WE HAVE OVER DEATH.

SOME DEATHS HAPPEN BY ACCIDENT, AND SOME WITH INTENTION, VIOLENCE, OR HATE. HOW DO WE EMOTIONALLY BALANCE DEATHS THAT DEMAND OUTRAGE AND PERSONAL HEALING AT THE SAME TIME?

SOME DEATHS ARE NOT EASY TO MAKE PEACE WITH, AND IT MIGHT NOT BE POSSIBLE.

THE PRACTICE OF SPEAKING AND THINKING ABOUT DEATH DOES NOT MAKE ACCEPTING DEATH EASY OR PAINLESS.

THE PEOPLE AROUND US BECOME PART OF US. THEY'RE STORED IN MEMORIES THAT ARE ENCODED IN OUR NEURAL NETWORKS, SOMETIMES PERSISTING BEYOND THEIR LIFE. WHEN THOSE PEOPLE DIE, THEY REMAIN PART OF OUR PHYSICAL BEINGS.

THOSE MEMORY PATHWAYS CAN BECOME LESS AND LESS USED OVER TIME, MAKING IT HARDER TO REACH THOSE PEOPLE IN OUR MINDS, BUT THEY STILL LIVE DOWN THE PATHWAYS, JUST A LITTLE LONGER OF A THOUGHT-WALK TO REACH THEM.

SPENDING TIME DOING WHAT WE LOVE GAINS MEANING BECAUSE THE TIME WE ARE DEDICATING TO THOSE THINGS IS LIMITED. IF WE HAD UNLIMITED TIME TO SPEND WITH OUR FRIENDS, OUR FAMILIES, OUR LOVES, OR OUR ANIMALS, WOULD THE TIME SPENT FEEL SPECIAL OR IMPORTANT? IF THERE WAS NO SCARCITY, WOULD WE BECOME BORED BY WHAT ONCE BROUGHT JOY AND PURPOSE?

WHAT THINGS DO YOU NEED IN YOUR LIFE TO FEEL FULFILLED?

IF YOU COME TO A DECISION POINT IN THE FUTURE—TREATING TERMINAL ILLNESS, FINDING CARE FOR ELDERS, UNDERGOING RISKY MEDICAL PROCEDURES—WHAT THINGS DO YOU NEED IN ORDER TO MAKE BEING ALIVE FEEL MEANINGFUL?

READING A BOOK?

TALKING WITH FRIENDS OR CARING FOR A PET?

WHAT THINGS CAN YOU LIVE WITHOUT?

WE OFTEN DON'T TALK ABOUT WHAT WE WANT FROM LIFE IN THE CONTEXT OF DEATH AND EFFORTS TO PROLONG LIFE.

WE HAVE "DO NOT RESUSCITATE" ORDERS AND MEDICAL DIRECTIVES — THINGS OUTLINING WHAT WE DON'T WANT DONE TO OUR BODIES — BUT WE FAIL TO DISCUSS WHAT THINGS ARE NECCESSARY TO HAVE FOR LIFE TO FEEL ALIVE.

IF WE DON'T SHARE WHAT WE WANT WITH OTHERS, WE ARE LESS INFORMED WHEN THE TIME COMES TO MAKE DECISIONS ABOUT OUR OWN AND OTHERS' OPTIONS AT END-OF-LIFE CARE OR MEDICAL INTERVENTION.

CLOSE YOUR EYES
AND IMAGINE
KNOWING

YOU HAVE
A
CERTAIN,
FINITE
AMOUNT
OF TIME
REMAINING
TO BE
ALIVE.
A YEAR,
LET'S SAY.

HOW
WOULD
YOU SPEND
THAT TIME?

IMAGINING THE FINITENESS
OF YOUR OWN LIFE
CAN ILLUMINATE THE THINGS THAT
FILL YOU WITH MEANING OR JOY.

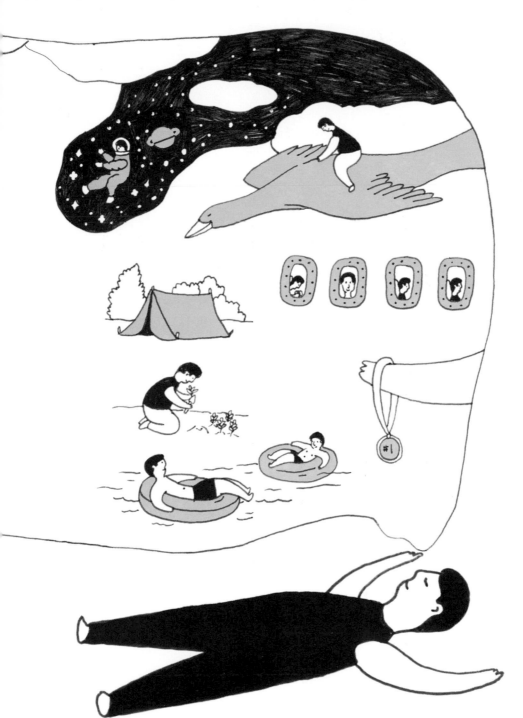

MOST OF US DON'T HAVE THE ABILITY OR DESIRE TO DROP EVERYTHING AND LIVE AS EXTRAVAGANTLY AS OUR IMAGINATIONS TAKE US, WHICH MAY BE ONE DIRECTION YOUR MIND GOES WHEN IMAGINING THE SCARCITY OF LIFE. BUT THINKING ABOUT OUR OWN DEATHS CAN ALLOW US TO FIND THE ASPECTS OF OUR LIVES THAT WE CAN CULTIVATE TO MAKE US FEEL LESS FEARFUL OF DEATH BECAUSE WE'RE ABLE TO HAVE A MORE FULL LIFE WHILE WE CAN

PREPARING YOURSELF TO NO LONGER BE IS A LIFELONG PROCESS. PREPARING FOR OURSELVES AND OTHERS TO LEAVE US IS A PROCESS WE CAN BEGIN WITH EACH OTHER — TO TALK ABOUT WHAT IT MEANS TO DIE, WHAT IT MEANS TO LIVE, HOW WE AFFECT EACH OTHER, AND WHAT THINGS WE NEED TO EXIST IN A FULL LIFE.

WE WILL SPEND INFINITELY MORE TIME DEAD THAN WE EVER SPENT ALIVE.
LET'S TALK ABOUT OUR FEARS AND SORROWS, OUR ANGER AND OUR ANXIETIES.

DYING IS NOT FAILING.

DEATH IS SORROWFUL
        AND HORRIBLE
        AND LOVING
        AND NATURAL
        AND NORMAL.

WE GET TO BE HERE
FOR OUR LIVES.

WE ARE ALLOWED TO
BREATHE AND FIND JOY
AND PAIN AND LOVE,
AND THOSE THINGS ARE THE
GIFT WE ARE GIVEN WITH
THE KNOWLEDGE THAT AT
THE END OF IT, WE WILL DIE.

WE WOULD NEVER
GET TO LIVE

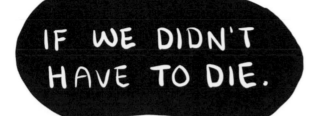

ACKNOWLEDGMENTS

Thanks to Kate, agent extraordinaire, for helping bring this death book to life. To Lauren for helping make the vision cohesive and impactful. To Stella for comforting me while I cried about death. To my friends for giving valuable feedback and insight during the process. To every creature who has died in the process of making this earth and to those who have lost their lives due to human harm. To all the people who have lost their lives in tragic or loving or peaceful or sudden ways and to the people who survived the grief of those losses. We are all in the mystery of life together, and we will all be in the mystery of death together.

ABOUT THE AUTHOR

IRIS GOTTLIEB is an author and illustrator from Durham, North Carolina. She has authored three books, *Seeing Science*, *Seeing Gender*, and *Natural Attraction*, and illustrated ten books on a wide range of subjects, from the science of pop music to sustainable food practices. She works to make information more engaging and accessible through drawing and approachable writing. Her prized possession is over five thousand shark teeth collected on the beaches of North Carolina.